Exploring the Occult

ANGELS and DEMONS

Stuart A. Kallen

San Diego, CA

© 2024 ReferencePoint Press, Inc.
Printed in the United States

For more information, contact:
ReferencePoint Press, Inc.
PO Box 27779
San Diego, CA 92198
www.ReferencePointPress.com

ALL RIGHTS RESERVED.
No part of this work covered by the copyright hereon may be reproduced or used in any form or by any means—graphic, electronic, or mechanical, including photocopying, recording, taping, web distribution, or information storage retrieval systems—without the written permission of the publisher.

LIBRARY OF CONGRESS CATALOGING-IN-PUBLICATION DATA

Names: Kallen, Stuart A., author.
Title: Angels and demons / by Stuart A. Kallen.
Description: San Diego, CA : ReferencePoint Press, [2024] | Series: Exploring the occult | Includes bibliographical references and index. |
Identifiers: LCCN 2023041181 (print) | ISBN 9781678207120 (library binding) | ISBN 9781678207137 (ebook)
Subjects: LCSH: Angels and demons--Juvenile literature-- Parapsychology--Juvenile literature.

Contents

Introduction — 4
Spirits in the Sky

Chapter One — 8
Everlasting Angels

Chapter Two — 20
Guardian Angels

Chapter Three — 32
Harnessing Angelic Energy

Chapter Four — 43
Devils and Demons

Source Notes — 54
For Further Research — 57
Index — 59
Picture Credits — 63
About the Author — 64

Introduction

Spirits in the Sky

Most people are familiar with the superheroes of the DC Universe, including Superman, Batman, and Wonder Woman. Fewer might be aware that some characters in the DC Universe are based on angels found in the Bible. Zauriel is an angel who left heaven to join the Justice League and serve humanity. Michael Demiurgos is an archangel, or chief angel, who battles bad guys aided by his half-human, half-angel daughter, Elaine Belloc. The Marvel Cinematic Universe has its own share of personalities based on angels, and similar beings can be found in Japanese manga and anime.

It is easy to see why comic creators love angels. People across most religions and cultures have long seen angels as divine superheroes. Like Zauriel, Demiurgos, and Belloc, angels are all-knowing, all-seeing, and all-powerful. They can fly, read minds, and according to the Bible, are "greater in might and power"[1] than humans. Biblical angels can create something from nothing, warp time, and control reality itself. And like modern superheroes, angels crush evil, protect the innocent, and promote justice.

The archangel Michael is the Superman of the Bible. Dressed in armor and wielding a dazzling sword, Michael single-handedly vanquishes demons, dragons, and entire armies. Archangel Uriel is another heroic biblical being. He holds the sun in the palm of his hand and wields power over thunder, lightning, and earthquakes.

If angels are divine superheroes, demons reign as the ultimate biblical supervillains. Satan, the most potent symbol of evil, rebels against all that is good and true. Commanding an army of demons, Satan rules the damned as the prince of hell. Satan is said to be a fallen angel, thrown down to earth after rebelling against God. He is referred to as the lord of the demons throughout the second part of the Bible, the New Testament. The horned Satan with his cloven hooves can inflict sickness on the innocent and corrupt the devout with an endless stream of lies.

The archangel Michael singlehandedly vanquishes demons, dragons, and entire armies. Much like modern-day superheroes, angels can warp time, crush evil, protect the innocent, and promote justice.

According to Jewish folklore, lesser demons also possess superpowers. They can fly from one end of the earth to the other, and they can see into the future. Demons with similar powers can be found in traditional cultures in which malevolent spirits need to be appeased with gifts and prayers lest they prey on the innocent. Such beliefs have produced countless customs meant to deflect or tame demons.

Divine Energies

Angels and demons are most often linked to what are called the Abrahamic religions: Judaism, Christianity, and Islam. But as Christian religious philosopher Thomas Aquinas wrote in the thirteenth century, "Angels transcend every religion, every philosophy, every creed. In fact, angels have no religion as we know it . . . their existence precedes every religious system that has existed on earth."[2]

Thomas was so focused on the nature of angels that he is known as the Angelic Doctor. His interest was undoubtedly piqued by the prominent role that angels play in the Bible. Angels and demons are also mentioned frequently in the Koran and in the teachings of Sikhism and the Bahá'í faith. The supernatural spirits are also popular with those who do not practice any formal religion. As spiritual coach Gabby Bernstein writes, "Angels are nondenominational and will help you in whatever spiritual or religious form resonates with you. And while they're often depicted in human form, you can envision them in any way you wish."[3]

> "Angels are nondenominational and will help you in whatever spiritual or religious form resonates with you."[3]
>
> —Gabby Bernstein, spiritual coach

In the Bible angels and demons are mainly connected to important events, such as the birth of Jesus. But day-to-day angelic interventions seem to be commonplace in the modern world. Believers say angels can influence nearly every aspect of life and death. Angels can be consulted to solve mundane problems with family relationships, love affairs, and business decisions. They can avert disasters, heal the sick, allow people to talk to the dead, or even provide a way to see into the future. If the hundreds of stories about angelic encounters found in books and online are true, angels are everywhere all the time. And they can help anyone and everyone in crisis.

Good Versus Evil

Angels and demons might represent opposite ends of the spectrum, but all their deeds—good and bad—are based on human behavior. Each person has the capacity to show angelic behavior such as compassion, mercy, and love. People also possess the ability to commit the most horrible, demonic deeds imaginable. But most people strive to be angelic; nearly 70 percent of Americans said they believed in angels, according to a 2023 Gallup poll. Nearly half say people who die and go to heaven become angels. As long as angels are seen as heavenly messengers and demons are viewed as Satan's consorts, the angelic side of human nature will act as a counterweight to those who seek to do the devil's bidding.

Chapter One

Everlasting Angels

Angels have been portrayed in countless works of art over the centuries. Radiant male and female angels are depicted with wings and surrounded by halos of light. They are shown wearing long white robes to symbolize the clouds, purity, and heaven. Chubby baby angels with wings, known as cherubs, are also popular subjects for artists. These calming images, some of which originated more than five hundred years ago, are what most people imagine when they think of angels.

Enter the internet and the world of memes. Starting in the late 2010s and continuing right up through today intriguing and often bizarre images of angels have been circulating on the internet and social media paired with the meme *biblically accurate angels*. The images looked nothing like the blissful beings seen on thousands of paintings and sculptures found in art museums. Some of the strangest angel images were based on biblical visions of angels called cherubim, as described by the prophet Ezekiel. According to Ezekiel, cherubim looked like "a wheel within a wheel . . . the wheels . . . were filled with eyes all around."[4] Images of intertwined golden wheels covered with eerie-looking eyes were shared hundreds of thousands of times in internet posts. Other biblically accurate cherubim were based on Ezekiel's descriptions of an angel bearing four faces—of a lion, an ox, a man, and an eagle. The angel had six large wings, four to cover its

Angels are most often depicted as blissful beings with wings but in some widely circulated images, angels look more like intersecting wheels covered with eyes.

faces and feet and two used to fly. Blogger Shawna Smith writes that as a result of the biblically accurate angels memes, "more and more individuals became acquainted with the fact that their depiction of angels might be entirely misinformed."[5]

Ancient Angels

Memes have not replaced traditional images of angels, however. Tens of thousands of drawings, paintings, and photos of ethereal humanoid creatures with harps, horns, halos, and wings still grace the internet. These traditional views, thousands of years in the making, remain extremely popular.

The first known figure said to be an angel was carved into a stone column around 4000 BCE in Sumer (present-day Iraq). The ancient Sumerian angel

> "More and more individuals [have become] acquainted with the fact that their depiction of angels might be entirely misinformed."[5]
>
> —Shawna Smith, blogger

9

was a messenger of God that had come down from heaven to pour the water of life into a king's cup. The Sumerians believed that each person had a protective spirit, similar to a guardian angel, that traveled with them everywhere. Sumerian artists depicted these entities, known as *kuribi*, with human heads, birdlike wings, and animal bodies. Individual Sumerians had altars in their homes to honor their personal *kuribi*, and these beings were the focus of poetry, paintings, and religious teachings.

Winged spirits of the heavens were also revered by the ancient Egyptians, who began building pyramids on the banks of the Nile River around 2500 BCE. The Egyptians were polytheists—they worshipped hundreds of gods and goddesses, many of them with angelic qualities. For example, the goddess Maat stood for truth, justice, and morality. Maat, sometimes depicted with feathered wings on each arm, ensured that only the righteous could enter the heavenly paradise after death. The mother goddess Isis, one of the most important Egyptian deities, was also depicted with angel-like wings. Like a guardian angel, Isis used her wings to enfold and protect people as they slept. The Egyptians believed that other angel-like creatures visited the dead to provide them with help in the afterlife. This led Egyptians to build small windows into tombs so angelic spirits could enter.

Archangels in Persia

Around the tenth century BCE, a new religion arose in Persia, in present-day Iran. Zoroastrianism was the first monotheistic religion—followers worship a single, all-powerful god. The origin story of the religion features an archangel. According to legend, an archangel named Vohu Manah contacted a mystic named Zoroaster, or Zarathustra. Vohu Manah, whose name means "good thoughts," was nine times the size of an average person. The archangel helped Zoroaster leave his body and travel to a heavenly paradise occupied by the god Ahura Mazda, known as the lord of light and wisdom. Ahura Mazda taught Zoroaster divine wisdom that was used to found Zoroastrianism.

Angelic Images

Some of the most famous paintings and sculptures of angels were created during the Renaissance era, which began in the 1300s and ended in the early 1600s. Since most people were illiterate at that time, churches filled their walls, ceilings, and stained glass windows with Bible stories, including those that revolved around angels. Renaissance artists largely sought to inspire religious fervor with their depictions of angels.

While seraphim are the only angels described with wings in the Bible, Renaissance artists began painting all angels with wings as a way to distinguish them from humans in artwork. Wings also gave angels a supernatural appearance while providing a way for them to fly to and from heaven. The gender of angels also began to change during the Renaissance. Scenes depicting the birth of Jesus often show angels with female features. The archangel Gabriel was sometimes depicted as either a woman or androgynous, with the features of both male and female. However they were depicted, Renaissance artists portrayed angels in idealized human form, dressed in exquisite gowns, with the glorious wings of eagles and swans.

Ahura Mazda created six archangels to assist humanity. One archangel named Asha Vahishta is called the spirit of righteousness and lord of sacred fires. This spirit ordered Zoroaster to protect the sacred divine fire and all other fires that warm people on earth. Other archangels represent plants, soil, metals, and waters. Together these archangels, called Amesha Spenta, represent different aspects of Ahura Mazda and act as the foundation of the universe.

The Zoroastrian faith includes a multitude of other angels. The Amesha Spenta are assisted by a group of twenty-three angels, who are either Yazata (meaning "worthy of worship") or Yazad (meaning "divine"). These angels are associated with various aspects of society, including divine wisdom, victory, charity, peace, health, riches, cattle, happiness, and morality. Another group is described as guardian angels. They are weapon-bearing, armor-clad warriors who protect and guide believers.

Righteous Angels

An estimated 120,000 people worldwide practiced Zoroastrianism in 2023. One of the underlying tenets of their faith is the belief

> "Fighting the good fight, a purpose of existing to do good, to make the world flourish, to work together, to respect and love each other . . . all that goes back to Zarathustra."[6]
>
> —Jamsheed Choksy, professor of central Eurasian studies

that the universe consists of two opposing forces: good and evil. Zoroastrians believe that good angels will someday battle bad angels. After the cataclysmic combat, individuals will be judged as either worthy or sinful by the divine spirit.

The monotheism of Zoroastrianism, with its emphasis on good versus evil, helped form the roots of Judaism, Christianity, and Islam. According to professor of central Eurasian studies Jamsheed Choksy, "You have these ideas that have fundamentally shaped Western society. . . . Fighting the good fight, a purpose of existing to do good, to make the world flourish, to work together, to respect and love each other . . . all that goes back to Zarathustra."[6]

The idea of angel warriors punishing the sinful found its way into the Hebrew Bible, also known as the Tanakh, believed to have been written around the eighth century BCE. The earliest Hebrew scholars believed that God spoke directly to humans and intervened in their affairs. God was viewed as merciless when it came to punishing sinners. However, in the sixth century BCE, Jewish people living in the Middle East came under Persian rule. During this period, Jews adopted some aspects of the Zoroastrian worldview. God came to be seen as more merciful but removed from human affairs. In his place, righteous angels judged people's deeds and meted out punishment. Evil angels, or demons, took on destructive powers.

Angelic Triads

The Hebrew Bible ranks angels in a celestial hierarchy in which some are seen as more important than others. This hierarchy was adopted by Christians in the second part of the Bible, the New Testament, which also discusses the life and teachings of Jesus. Today the Old and New Testaments are simply referred to as the Bible.

The Bible gives the names of nine groups of angels but does not specify their ranks or heavenly duties. That changed in the thirteenth century, when Thomas Aquinas arranged the angels into three hierarchies called triads. Each triad was broken down into three orders or choirs. The position of the angel in the hierarchy determined its jobs, the length of time it spent on earth, and its interaction with people and other angels.

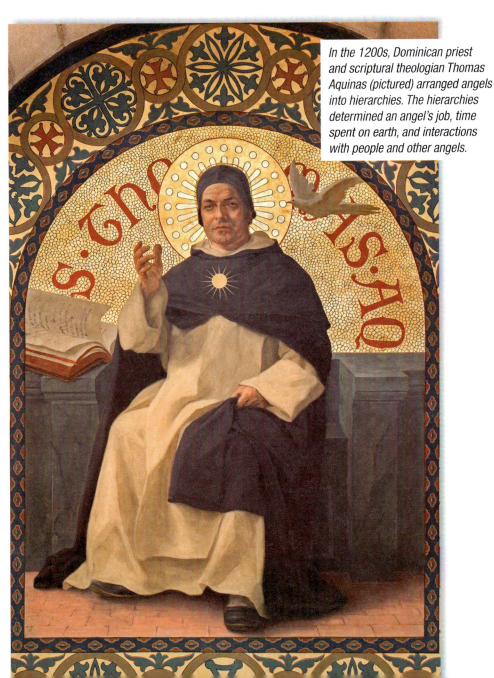

In the 1200s, Dominican priest and scriptural theologian Thomas Aquinas (pictured) arranged angels into hierarchies. The hierarchies determined an angel's job, time spent on earth, and interactions with people and other angels.

The top triad, called Angels of Pure Contemplation, consists of seraphim, cherubim, and thrones. These high-ranking angels spend most of their time in communion with God. The highest order of angels, seraphim are the only biblical angels said to have wings. Seraphim are based on the Zoroastrian angels of fire and known as fiery serpents. They are described as representing the four winds or directions, north, south, east, and west. Each seraphim has sixteen faces that are as bright as the rising sun. Their light is so intense that even other angels cannot look upon it.

Cherubim are the second-most powerful angels. A cherub is a single cherubim, from the Hebrew *kerub*, meaning "fullness of knowledge" or "one who intercedes." These angels who intervene in human affairs are the first angels mentioned in the Bible. In the book of Genesis, cherubim are placed at the entrance to the Garden of Eden to prevent Adam and Eve from returning after God evicts them. According to Doreen Virtue, author of more than twenty books on angels, thrones "are the bridge between the material and the spiritual, and represent God's fairness and justice."[7]

Devas in India

Around 80 percent of people in India practice Hinduism. Hindus believe that all living things—including plants, animals, and people—have angelic beings called devas that guard them and help them thrive. All are said to be the children or grandchildren of Brahma, the creator god. Hindus believe that there are thousands of different types of devas. They range from tiny sprites that are guardians of the smallest wildflowers to massive archangels that protect the sun. Other devas exist throughout the infinite universe.

Devas were first described in the Vedas, religious texts that originated in India around 1500 BCE. The term *devas* translates to "beings of light or radiance." These angels, which are found everywhere, are said to have achieved spiritual enlightenment. Religion editor Whitney Hopler provides context: "Light is often associated with wisdom. The word 'enlighten' means to give knowledge or understanding (especially spiritual insights) to someone. . . . Spiritually, light stands for truth from the good side of the spiritual realm overcoming lies from the evil side of the spiritual realm."

Whitney Hopler, "The Spiritual Meaning of Light in Angels and Miracles," Learn Religions, December 29, 2018. www.learnreligions.com.

The middle triad, Angels of the Cosmos, is made up of angels called dominions, virtues, and powers. Dominions, also known as lords, are said to oversee other angels and interpret God's commands. Dominions rule over earthly kingdoms and determine the outcome of wars. Dominions often appear in human form, riding red horses on battlefields. They are also described as wearing crowns, golden robes, and green stoles. The virtues are beneath the dominions and carry out their instructions. In this role, the virtues create miracles on earth and give powers to humans that help strengthen them for difficult tasks. Virtues are described as wearing priestly garments and carrying roses. Powers have sway over evil forces, preventing them from doing harm.

Archangels and Angels

Beings in the lowest angelic triad, Angels of the World, are called principalities, archangels, and angels. These spirits are said to live among people and are most likely to intervene in human affairs. The principalities, or princedoms, are closest in appearance to people and watch over the visible human world. They are described as having princely powers to rule over the welfare of cities, states, and nations. In the Old Testament these angels are referred to as the Prince of Persia and the Prince of Greece, both rulers with supernatural powers. They have been depicted wearing princely robes, golden belts, and crowns.

Archangels are ranked on the second-lowest tier of the angelic hierarchy. Only two archangels are mentioned in the Old Testament. Michael is the warrior of heaven, and Gabriel is a heavenly messenger. These archangels are recognized in Judaism, Christianity, and Islam. Other biblical characters recognized as archangels are mentioned in what are called Apocryphal texts. These are religious works that were included in earlier versions of the Bible but are now considered of secondary importance. For example, an Apocryphal Old Testament text called the book of Tobit discusses Raphael as God's healer. This leads Catholics and Lutherans to view Raphael as an archangel. Similarly, Apocryphal

Russian Orthodox and Anglican texts describe the archangel Uriel, who is said to watch over the world and the lowest part of hell.

Archangels are central to the New Testament, where they act as ministers of God and agents of revelation. The archangel Gabriel, for example, appears to Mary as a traditional angelic messenger, informing her that the child she will give birth to is Jesus. Lesser angels herald the birth of Jesus, witness his ascent into heaven, and prophesy his return.

Angels occupy the lowest order of the angelic hierarchy. These beings are said to watch over every person. Angels sing God's praises in a heavenly court and serve as an army of a thousand warriors. Angels announce births, assign humans divine tasks, and communicate God's words to prophets. Angels also act as teachers and heavenly guides, interpreting prophecies and explaining holy visions.

Angels in the Bible were not described as having wings. Sometimes they were indistinguishable from humans, as the New Testament letter to the Hebrews says: "Do not neglect hospitality to strangers—for in doing so some have entertained angels without knowing it."[8] In other cases angels were described as creatures of incredible beauty, appearing as brilliant beams of light, blazing lightning, or precious stones. These beings did not need wings to fly between heaven and earth. They might climb up and down ladders or appear in a blazing fire.

Angels Mete Out Punishment

Perhaps the most dramatic role angels play in the New Testament is in the fight to defend good and vanquish evil. This graphic confrontation is described in Revelation, the last book of the Bible. It foretells the return of Jesus, the end of the world, and the establishment of a new heaven on earth. In Revelation sinners are punished and the righteous are allowed to enter a new heavenly city.

The book of Revelation, said to be written by John the Evangelist, begins with angels delivering a message from God. Throughout the twenty-two chapters of Revelation, angels mete out spectacular punishments. In chapter 8, seven angels with seven trumpets wreak havoc on earth. One angel fills an incense burner with fire and throws it down to earth, causing lightning, thunder, and earthquakes. This is followed by "hail and fire mingled with blood. . . . A third of the earth was burned up, a third of the trees were burnt up, and all green grass was burnt up."[9] This angel also caused the sea to flow red with blood and a star to fall and burn up rivers.

In Revelation 8:12 a fourth angel sounds its trumpet, causing one-third of the sun and stars to turn black. Later, seven angels deliver seven plagues to earth as the archangel Michael fights Satan and commands angel warriors in a final conflict between good and evil. In the last chapters of Revelation, angels show John the Evangelist a new holy city on earth, where the river of life flows crystal clear.

Angels of Islam

The book of Revelation is thought to have been written around 95 CE. About six centuries later, a new holy book was written based on the words of an archangel. People of the Islamic faith believe that the archangel Gabriel revealed God's messages to the Prophet Muhammad in the early seventh century. These revelations were recorded in the Koran over the course of twenty-three years. When the message was finalized, Islam spread rapidly across the Middle East and Central Asia, with angels playing major roles.

Islam also has a hierarchy of angels. The top angels are most important as throne bearers of Allah, or God. They are symbolized by a man, a bull, an eagle, and a lion. The next order of angels consists of cherubim who praise Allah. The lower rank beneath cherubim consists of archangels: Jibril (Gabriel), the revealer; Mikal (Michael), the provider; Izra'il, the angel of death; and Israfil, the angel of the Last Judgment.

The Koran describes lesser angels called djinni (also spelled jinni or genies). Djinni were created from smokeless fire and have

In Islam, angels called djinni can influence people and perform magical deeds. In the famous tale from The Arabian Nights, a boy named Aladdin rubs a magic lamp. A djinn appears and must grant the boy's wishes.

no bodies. But they can appear in many forms through the use of illusion. In their many guises, djinni can appear as snakes, dogs, black cats, toads, or humans. Djinni can influence people in both positive and negative ways. Some are wicked; they are sworn to lead humans into sin by temptation. Others perform magical deeds to grant wishes meant to help humans improve their lives or satisfy their desires.

Djinni are said to be as plentiful as grains of sand and can cause shooting stars and violent sandstorms. The most famous djinn is described in the tale of Aladdin in *The Arabian Nights*. This spirit appears when the poor boy Aladdin rubs a magic lamp. This angel is obligated to grant Aladdin wishes, and the boy becomes a rich and powerful ruler.

> "[Angels] are bringers of wisdom, compassion, strength, and love not as a reward, but as a reminder. A reminder of the Divine Presence in this world and, more importantly, our responsibility to revere and protect it."[10]
>
> —Daniel N. Geffen, rabbi

Listen to the Angels

Angels give believers a sense of certainty in an uncertain world. They are seen as personal guardians, holy avengers, and beings that hold the key to success. These beliefs are contradicted by those who argue that the world has changed beyond recognition since the Bible and other holy books were written, making angels irrelevant in modern times. But Rabbi Daniel N. Geffen writes that angels still have an important role to play, one that they have played for millennia:

> We are currently living in a world that is frustratingly intent on its own destruction. It is all too easy to throw up our hands and pray for an answer to come from the heavens; but this is not enough. The angels of our tradition are messengers, not problem solvers. . . . They are bringers of wisdom, compassion, strength, and love not as a reward, but as a reminder. A reminder of the Divine Presence in this world and, more importantly, our responsibility to revere and protect it, in all its forms.[10]

Chapter Two

Guardian Angels

It may be hard for some individuals to believe that a powerful, invisible force watches over them and protects them from evil. But polls taken over the years consistently show that around half of all Americans believe that they have a personal guardian angel. The percentage is even higher (more than 75 percent) among Roman Catholics. These numbers are reflected in the countless stories about guardian angels that can be found on social media and in traditional media. It is said that guardian angels ward off evil, provide guidance, and offer special protection to those who perform good deeds.

The Bible does not explicitly mention angels that protect individuals, but believers interpret several biblical passages as proof that guardian angels exist. In the Old Testament, God says to Moses, "Now go, lead the people to the place I spoke of, and my angel will go before you."[11] Believers also quote fourth-century Christian theologian Saint Jerome, who wrote, "How great the dignity of the soul, since each one has from his birth an angel commissioned to guard it."[12] This conviction has been reinforced by many religious leaders over the centuries, including Pope Pius XII, who stated in 1958:

> Everyone, no matter how humble he may be, has angels to watch over him. They are heavenly, pure and splendid, and yet they have been given us to

keep us company on our way: they have been given the task of keeping careful watch over you. . . . And not only do they want to protect you from the dangers which waylay you throughout your journey: they are actually by your side, helping your souls as you strive.[13]

> "Not only do [angels] want to protect you from the dangers which waylay you throughout your journey: they are actually by your side, helping your souls as you strive."[13]
>
> —Pope Pius XII

Protected by Archangel Michael

Michael is the most powerful archangel in the Bible and the Koran and is viewed by some as a personal source of protection and spirituality. Michael is said to directly communicate with people to protect them from harm. He has exceptional strength, fights for good, and empowers believers with these traits when they are

Moses looks out across the Promised Land. In one passage in the Bible, God urges Moses to follow His angel as Moses leads the Jews to safety. This passage and others are cited as proof of the existence of guardian angels.

in trouble. Michael might offer guidance by speaking to a person directly. Sometimes his messages are soft, mystical, and difficult to understand. Other times Michael's words are loud and to the point. As blogger Hope Lux writes, "In some cases, this voice may feel like the booming sound of thunder. But other times, it may appear as a whisper from nowhere. However you hear him, know that his message always comes from a place of love."[14]

Some of those who say they have received messages from Michael report that an intense feeling of calm comes over them, accompanied by a warm sensation throughout the body. Archangels also are said to make their presence known through flashes of light. Michael is associated with bright blue or purple light, which represents his spiritual aura. Angel enthusiast Gabby Bernstein writes, "I often experience Archangel Michael's presence when I see a glimmer of blue light. Sometimes I can even feel his presence—it's like the room is expanding and a huge energy has come into the space. Michael makes himself known if you're open to experiencing him."[15]

Sometimes Michael leaves physical signs to reveal his presence. There have been numerous reports of Michael placing feathers in unusual places. A poster named Jen on Hope Lux's website says she has found over 150 purple feathers since the early 2010s. Some were hard to spot, behind the dog kennel or in the bushes. After being diagnosed with cancer in 2019, Jen writes she found three purple feathers in a single day, which she took as a message from her guardian angel Michael: "It was in that moment I knew the Universe had more for me to do, & I would get through this. That was 3 years ago, I am now well recovered and happy. I knew it was the angelic realm, it's nice to know it was Michael communicating and protecting [me] especially over that time. I am forever grateful for the Divine connection of guidance, love & light."[16]

Healed by Raphael

As Jen was fighting cancer, she looked to Michael as her guardian angel. Others seek protection from Raphael, the archangel most often associated with healing. Those who believe Raphael is visit-

Guardian Angel Caught on Camera

There are countless images posted on social media that are said to be guardian angels. Most are paintings or computer-generated imagery. But video-sharing platforms like TikTok and YouTube contain dozens of videos that seem to show real guardian angels caught on camara. One video, which went viral on Facebook and generated numerous TV news stories, was shot by a motion-sensor security camera at Glen Thorman's home in East Jordan, Michigan, in 2018. The camera caught what appears to be a white angel with outstretched wings hovering in the night sky above his truck. Moments later the angel flies off. Thorman sent a photo of the event to his church pastor, Deneille Moes, who said, "It was really clear to me the minute I looked at the photo, I just kind of freaked out a bit. I went like 'Whoa! That's an angel!' And I texted him back, 'That's an angel.' There wasn't any doubt in my mind that we were looking at something supernatural."

Quoted in Keith Darnay, "Angel Image Captured by Security Camera?," KTSM, May 14, 2018. www.ktsm.com.

---

ing them during times of illness or extreme stress seek signs that are said to reveal his presence. The archangel is associated with the color emerald green, and he might appear as a shimmer of light or a gentle orb in the peripheral vision. Raphael has also been seen as a green emanation of light, called an aura. This may appear around an entire person or near a body part that needs to heal. In some cases an aura could manifest itself along with a sensation of heat, tingling, chills, or other vibrations around an injured area. This happened to basketball coach Amanda Peart, who severely injured her hip during a game. Peart called on Raphael to heal her, and the reaction was immediate. She says her hands turned ice cold, then very hot and tingly. She felt the same sensation in her hip. Peart says that two hours later her hip was completely healed. Author Doreen Virtue, who described Peart's experiences, explains the miraculous cure:

> The tingling heat is undoubtedly the vast energy that Archangel Raphael generates and runs through the people whom he heals. It's like having a giant surge of electricity

course through you.... I believe that the tingles and vibrations are waves of Raphael's energy pulsating through the body, like healing laser beams. The vibrations undoubtedly push away toxins and open the body's passages for healthy blood and oxygen flow.[17]

Raphael is said to be able to heal more than the human body. With his emerald-green color, associated with the natural world, he is credited with inspiring people to heal nature and the environment. Those who believe they have been in contact with Raphael often have the urge to go for a hike or join an environmental organization. As a blogger with the username Wille explains:

Your angels always want what's best for you, but may have different ways of showing you that. Archangel Raphael watches out for our health and wellness, as well as the beauty of nature. It only makes sense that he would try to connect with you in this way. Whether you are enjoying more daily walks, hikes, or perhaps have taken up a new outdoor hobby, Archangel Raphael believes in the importance of your health and connection to the outside world.... You may find meditative walks in nature to be particularly soothing right now. If you are hoping to connect with Archangel Raphael, doing it in nature certainly won't hurt![18]

Ariel's Connection to Nature

The name Ariel, which means "lion of God" in Hebrew, is another archangel associated with healing and nature. The archangel is said to work closely with Raphael when providing cures for physical problems. Ariel has traditionally been depicted in male form, but in recent times the archangel is often represented as female. An online psychic who goes by the name Stacey writes that Ariel is the guardian angel of Mother Earth: "She is most widely known for overseeing the natural world. She can help deepen your relationship with animals, natural elements like wind and water, and plants. Being so entwined with Mother Nature allows Archangel Ariel to help us in grounding and connecting with the Earth in order to receive abundance and manifest physical desires."[19]

> "Being so entwined with Mother Nature allows Archangel Ariel to help us in grounding and connecting with the Earth in order to receive abundance and manifest physical desires."[19]
>
> —Stacey, online psychic

Ariel is associated with the color pink, which is said to represent love and peace. She may be called on to provide mental and physical strength. Ariel's connection with nature also makes her the guardian angel of plants and animals, including pets and those living in the wild. As nature's healer, Ariel is said to guard the earth's resources, including forests, rivers, and oceans. Stacey says she connected with Ariel while on a camping trip in the wilderness. While she was meditating next to a peaceful stream, a beautiful blue and yellow butterfly perched on her knee. Stacey says she greeted the butterfly and "immediately received a download—an image in my mind. Archangel Ariel has joined me in the form of this butterfly! She didn't speak to me with words. Instead, she filled me with such unconditional love, and an energy of responsibility for my purpose. My body was warm, 'buzzy' all over, and I felt like I was glowing from the inside out."[20] The butterfly remained on Stacey's knee for more than thirty minutes.

Messages from Gabriel

Gabriel is another archangel said to appear in both masculine and feminine forms. As the archangel who announced the birth of Jesus, Gabriel is now known as the guardian angel of writers, teachers, and public speakers who need to communicate clearly. In the Bible, Gabriel also delivers prophetic messages about future events. This leads believers to call on the archangel when they need help concerning careers, business endeavors, romance, and other major life choices.

Gabriel has long been depicted in literature and art as blowing a horn on Judgment Day. This association links Gabriel to the color copper or brass. Because of Gabriel's association with the horn, some musicians and performance artists call on the archangel for career guidance.

Gabriel might deliver help and inspiration through visions and recurring thoughts. Authors Linda Miller-Russo and Peter Miller-Russo recommend concentrating on Gabriel before falling asleep at night: "You should awaken with a dream-world memory that contains the solution (or a seed to the solution) to your problem. Sometimes you will not remember having a dream at all. Yet the answer to the problem will come to your conscious awareness later in the day."[21]

Fiery Angel Wisdom

While Gabriel is often depicted holding a horn, the archangel Uriel can be seen in artwork carrying a book or scroll. This is based on the idea that Uriel is the spirit of wisdom, enlightenment, and spiritual growth. He is said to bring clarity to confusing situations and provide insight to those who are making important decisions. Uriel's name translates to "fire of God," and the archangel can shine a heavenly light to ward off darkness, ignorance, and evil. This spiritual light has healing powers, according to wellness blogger Lynda: "When Archangel Uriel is around, you may feel a sudden sense of calmness and serenity. This is because his presence brings a sense of peace and tranquility."[22]

Uriel is associated with the colors red and gold, which represent his fiery powers. People turn to Uriel when they need help overcoming addiction, depression, anxiety, and anger. According to author Ambika Wauters, "Archangel Uriel helps us live our worthiness and find our free-

> "When Archangel Uriel is around, you may feel a sudden sense of calmness and serenity. This is because his presence brings a sense of peace and tranquility."[22]
>
> —Lynda, wellness blogger

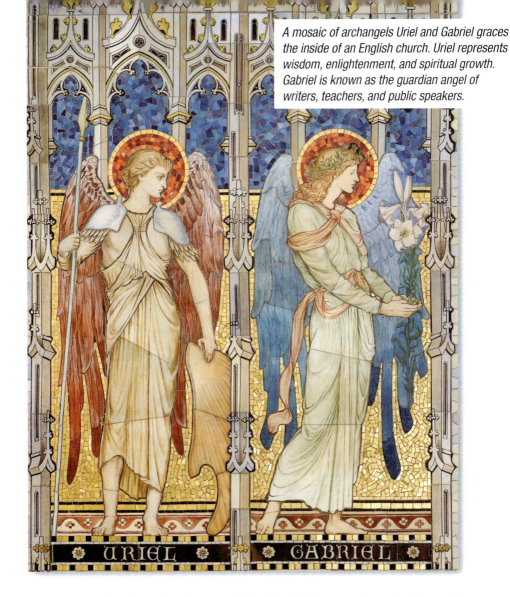

A mosaic of archangels Uriel and Gabriel graces the inside of an English church. Uriel represents wisdom, enlightenment, and spiritual growth. Gabriel is known as the guardian angel of writers, teachers, and public speakers.

dom from abusive situations which diminish our value. Archangel Uriel heals any loss of self-respect. He helps us find empowerment in our own value so we can shine our light on to the world and claim our good."[23]

Angels Without Names

Believers who need to navigate difficult situations might seek spiritual and emotional aid from the most well-known archangels. But sometimes unnamed angels seem to appear out of nowhere when there is trouble. Believers claim that these guardian angels

One believer credits a guardian angel with saving his life. He says he would have stepped on a deadly black mamba (pictured) while on vacation in South Africa if not for the voice that told him to not take another step.

intervene to prevent nearly every type of accident and tragedy. Angels have been said to heal the sick and rescue those nearing death. These stories, which are often posted on social media or discussion websites like Reddit, often lack details such as the date or location and are impossible to verify. However, those who make such claims have little doubt that their lives have been touched by guardian angels.

    A Reddit poster known as Lightenergy says he was on vacation in South Africa when he went for a swim by a beautiful waterfall. He got cold and decided to walk over to a warm patch of grass to dry off. Lightenergy says he was about to step over a log when he heard a booming masculine voice telling him to stop. He looked around and saw that he was alone. Then he noticed a deadly black mamba snake very close to his big toe. The snake, Lightenergy writes,

> was waiting to see what my next move was to be, and he had seen me long before I saw him. I slowly backed up and walked very carefully backwards. . . . I have no explanation for the voice that I heard, except that it was

so loud and was inside my head rather than heard with my ears, and it came at a time when I didn't feel in any danger at all—in fact I was very calm and happy. I feel that it was my guardian angel who shouted at me to stop, as I would have stepped right on the snake. My guardian angel saved my life.[24]

A rock climber who goes by the username Reedkeeper makes a similar claim. Reedkeeper says he was climbing a steep cliff face when his left handhold broke free. He grasped with his right hand but failed to get a handhold. He says:

> You know that feeling when you are tilting back in a chair and you tilt just a little too far? That's exactly what I felt. I started to fall backwards and everything got real slow. I knew I was going to die or at best be crippled. I felt a hand gently press against my back, right between my shoulder blades. It felt like a perfectly normal right hand and it pushed me back against the rock face. I took a moment to steady myself, I was pretty shaken up, and then I climbed down to safety.[25]

Reedkeeper, who says he does not use drugs and was not on any medication, believes a guardian angel stopped him from falling and in all likelihood saved his life.

Accidents and Angels

Guardian angels are often seen by people who are involved in car crashes. In some cases angels provide much-needed help in dire situations. Arika Stovall says she was aided by an angel in 2016 when she experienced a horrific crash with her boyfriend, Hunter Hanks, at the wheel.

Hanks was driving his Toyota pickup truck on a Florida freeway at 85 miles per hour (137 kph) when he lost control of the vehicle.

A Guardian Angel Leaves His Hat Behind

Guardian angels are known to leave objects behind, such as feathers or flowers. But a Reddit poster with the username Arielflip claims a guardian angel gave her a hat after she was in a serious early morning car wreck: "Out of nowhere, a guy shows up to my driver side window. He has a large cowboy hat on. He says, 'You are going to be okay,' and he holds my hand. I asked him his name and he looks away like he doesn't want to tell me. Then he says 'Bill Hill.' I smiled and said thank you. . . . [When the ambulance arrives] he moves out of the way for the EMT's to get me out of the car."

A few days after the crash, Arielflip found the cowboy hat in the back seat of her totaled car, which had been towed to a junkyard. Arielflip says she searched unsuccessfully for anyone named Bill Hill who might live in the region: "He never existed and we lived in a small town of only a few thousand at the time. . . . How did his hat get in my back seat? . . . I think he was an Angel! Why would I have his hat?"

Quoted in Melissa Brinks, "15 People Tell Eerie Stories of Guardian Angels Looking Out for Them," Ranker, March 2, 2021. www.ranker.com.

The truck hit a pole and was completely destroyed, nearly cut in half by the impact. Stovall looked over and saw that Hanks's head had gone through the windshield. He was covered in blood and not moving. Stovall says at that moment she saw a man bathed in bright light with a long white beard. No other cars or people were nearby. In a Facebook post, Stovall explained what happened next:

> He was my guardian angel. He saw me and immediately told me that an ambulance was coming. I jumped out of the car, ran over to Hunter's side and just looked at this man. . . . Here is the miracle part: no broken bones, concussions that lasted not even 24 hours, no internal damage, and just a few stitches in my knee and Hunter's face. . . . [We were] both already released from the hospital not even 48 hours after entering.[26]

Stovall believes her guardian angel helped maneuver the truck so that the pole missed both driver and passenger. She also says the angel attracted her gaze and helped distract her while emergency personnel cut and lifted Hanks out of the truck. "This man," she says, "looking at him for a short moment helped me not witness Hunter being peeled out of the truck. I believe if I saw that I would have had a heart attack. . . . I asked this man when the ambulance was coming. He told me in just a second. He walked away."[27]

Some might question why a guardian angel would allow Hanks to drive dangerously fast or would let the truck smash into a pole instead of steering it to safety. Stovall believes the crash was a sign from above, proof that her fate is predetermined by heavenly forces and that it was not time for her or Hanks to die. Stovall is among millions who believe angels can deliver guidance, enlightenment, and strength and even ward off death.

Belief is a powerful force that can help people overcome seemingly impossible odds and guide them in a crisis. No one has provided proof that mysterious cosmic entities watch over everyone. But those who say they have been helped by guardian angels seem empowered by their beliefs, and that seems to be all the proof they need.

Chapter Three

Harnessing Angelic Energy

When Damien Echols saw his first angel, he was in a hellish place, a cell in a maximum security prison in Arkansas. Echols was serving a life sentence after being wrongfully convicted of murdering three children in 1993. Ultimately, he was released from prison, after new DNA evidence proved his innocence. Before his release, Echols had a surprising encounter with what he is certain was an angel. "It wasn't like a person with blond hair and blue eyes and wings on its back," he says. It looked like "two black triangles: one big triangle as the body, and a smaller one for the head. It had no discernible facial features. But I knew it was an angel. And I got why angels in the Bible say 'be not afraid' whenever they show up, because this thing was terrifying."[28]

During his years in prison, Echols began practicing ceremonial magic (sometimes called ritual magic and sometimes spelled *magick*). Those who practice ceremonial magic conduct ceremonies that include chanting spells that are meant to influence events in their lives. Ceremonial magicians believe they can summon supernatural spirits, including angels, to help them improve their health, finances, and relationships. Echols says that when he was beaten by prison guards, he imagined archangels protecting his body. He conducted ceremonies in which he visualized his freedom. He credits these spiritual moments as leading to his eventual release from prison: "I performed magick to draw freedom toward me."[29]

Echols shares his supernatural discoveries through books, videos, and social media. One of his books, *Angels & Archangels*, describes the powers associated with angels and explains basic magical practices and rituals that readers can use to call on celestial beings. Echols also teaches magical techniques to others on social media. His YouTube videos, numbering close to ninety, had attracted more than 3 million views by 2023.

Reviving Ancient Beliefs

Ceremonial magic forms the basis of a belief system called Wicca that emerged in England in the late nineteenth century. Wiccans sometimes refer to themselves as pagans or neo-pagans, terms that define people whose beliefs do not conform to mainstream religious teachings. Pagan practices were drawn from the ancient Celts, who once populated the British Isles. People in the pre-Christian Celtic culture worshipped many nature-based gods and goddesses, including angel-like beings such as fairies, sprites, and gnomes. Author Jenny Smedley explains that these supernatural beings

> "[Wiccans] are not as in awe of angels as some more modern religious practitioners are, and treat them almost like friends and confidants, as if they are here to serve and help [them]."[30]
>
> —Jenny Smedley, author

might be seen as fairy-like creatures inhabiting trees or water, or any other natural feature, rather than flitting around among the clouds, but . . . they are nevertheless considered to be angels. . . . [Wiccans] are not as in awe of angels as some more modern religious practitioners are, and treat them almost like friends and confidants, as if they are here to serve and help [them] rather than be purely subservient to any one god.[30]

There are no specific rules concerning rituals, prayers, or methods for conducting ceremonial magic. Individuals who wish to

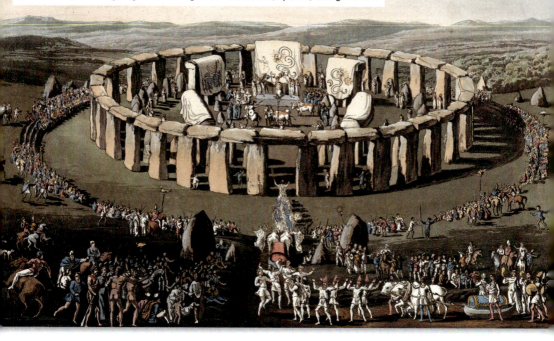

The ancient Celts (such as those who might have taken part in rituals at Stonehenge, pictured here) worshipped many nature-based gods and goddesses, including angel-like beings such as fairies, sprites, and gnomes.

harness angelic energy do so using whatever techniques feel right to them. Some simply focus their minds on their needs and call on the spirits for help. Others conduct elaborate ceremonies that can go on for hours. But the most common methods for conducting ceremonial magic, described in countless books and internet tutorials, involve working with some basic tools. And the practices are open to anyone, whatever their core spiritual or religious beliefs.

Setting Up an Altar

Most rituals are centered on raised structures or platforms called altars. Anything can be used as an altar, including a small table, a desk, or even a tree stump or flat stone. Altars are usually covered with a piece of fabric known as an altar cloth. Those seeking to harness angelic energy might choose a cloth that has prints of angels or clouds on it. Some embroider messages to the angels on their altar cloths. Others use whatever piece of cloth is pleasing to the eye, or they purchase one of the hundreds of altar cloths available on craft websites.

Other items placed on altars during rituals might include flowers, a chalice, an incense burner, and a wand. Altars usually hold three or more candles. Wiccans believe a white candle should always be present since it represents spiritual purity. Colored candles are also used. The colors depend on the purpose of the ritual and which angel is being summoned. For example, Ariel's color is pink, meaning a pink candle would be appropriate when calling on this archangel. A person hoping for angelic help with a relationship might use a red candle since that color is commonly used to symbolize love. Those seeking financial help might use a green candle to represent money.

Candles need to be placed in safe, fireproof candleholders. Lamps that burn different-colored oils are safer to work with and have special significance, according to Wiccan priestess Silver RavenWolf: "Oil lamps are very magickal. The treasured temple oil lamps of priests and priestesses of old represented the light of the divine in an otherwise dark world."[31]

Whatever choices a person makes setting up an altar, the process should not be stressful. According to RavenWolf, "What you find comfortable in your spirituality is right for you. If you want your altar to hold only an angel statue . . . then that's how it will be."[32]

> "What you find comfortable in your spirituality is right for you. If you want your altar to hold only an angel statue . . . then that's how it will be."[32]
>
> —Silver RavenWolf, Wiccan priestess

Angels of Earth, Air, Fire, and Water

Wiccans place a high value on the four elements—earth, air, fire, and water—and almost all of the named angels in Apocryphal writings and religious texts are associated with one or more element. For example, angels with earth associations include the well-known archangel Uriel, along with lesser-known angels such as Jehiel and Hariel.

The earth element signifies abundance, prosperity, and strength. Uriel and other earth angels are said to assist with divination, financial problems, and accumulation of wealth. Wiccan priestess Ellen Dugan says, "Appeal for the archangel Uriel's assistance regarding practical matters of prosperity, the harvest, and gardening."[33] Those who wish to visualize Uriel or other earth angels wear forest-green clothing when conducting rituals and use green candles and altar cloths. They also place earth symbols such as bowls containing dirt, salt, dried grains, or quartz crystals on their altars.

Angels generally associated with the air element include the popular archangel Raphael, along with the lesser-known beings Moriel and Chasan. It is said that air represents psychic abilities, creative thoughts, and dreams. Yellow clothing and candles are employed when summoning Raphael. Herbs or essential oils associated with the air element include those with clean, fresh fragrances such as lavender, rosemary, and peppermint. On an altar, air might be represented by feathers and wind instruments such as flutes and recorders.

The most powerful archangel, Michael, is associated with fire. Like the blazing sun, fire represents power, energy, and transformation. The color red, candles, swords, and knives represent fire on an altar. Spicey and strong-smelling herbs such as chili pepper, cinnamon, and cloves are often placed on an altar for spells meant to attract Michael.

Gabriel in the feminine form is the archangel of water. Gabriel is invoked by those hoping to purify their thoughts and overcome negative emotions. Water angels are summoned in ceremonies centered on love. Bowls of water are set on the altar, along with blue candles and stones such as turquoise and aquamarine. Apples, lettuce, and seaweed are also used to symbolize the water element.

Wiccans believe there is a fifth element, referred to as spirit, ether, or aether. This element, which is seen as a link between the physical and spiritual world, is represented by Metatron. This archangel is described in the apocryphal literature as a celestial scribe selected by God to write down his words. Wiccans see Metatron as a sort of superangel because he is said to have been the biblical

Wiccans view the archangel Metatron as a source of spiritual and intellectual inspiration. It is said that he was the biblical patriarch Enoch before ascending to the heavens and thus connects earth and heavenly energy. Pictured is one artist's vision of Metatron.

patriarch Enoch before ascending to the heavens. His connection with both earthly and heavenly energy means that Metatron can be drawn on as a source of spiritual and intellectual inspiration. A blogger with the username Whoismyguardianangel explains why believers call on Metatron: "Invoke Archangel Metatron when you're struggling to understand ancient esoteric wisdom. If you're new on the spiritual path and are seeking guidance, ask Archangel Metatron for help. . . . Archangel Metatron helps bring about a deepening of one's understanding of life's mystic secrets."[34]

Calling on Angels

It is common to start a ritual with a simple meditation that is meant to clear the mind of distracting day-to-day thoughts. This necessitates finding a quiet place, relaxing, closing the eyes, taking deep

Keeping Angels in Line

Author and Wiccan practitioner Damien Echols believes that there are strong differences between angels and archangels. He says angels are pure energy, while archangels are powerful forces that are meant to direct that energy. According to Echols, people need to be very specific when attempting to harness angelic energy:

> [Archangels] are everywhere—they're the very substance of which the cosmos is made. Archangels are essentially stars, just a couple steps down from gods. They exist on a level of creation immediately above ours, which makes them relatively easy to contact. They're also incredibly willing to work with us, if asked.
>
> Angels are more like elements—powerful energies with just enough intelligence to perform as directed. This is why you have to give them specific instructions, because they will typically accomplish a given task in the easiest way possible, and they aren't capable of discerning between human concepts of right and wrong. For this reason, I highly recommend telling them to do their work "in a way that harms none." It is also why magicians use archangels to guide and restrict angels to make sure that whatever magick they're doing with them manifests in beneficial ways.

Damien Echols, *Angels & Archangels: A Magician's Guide*. Boulder, CO: Sounds True, 2020, p. 15.

---

breaths, and focusing mental energy on the purpose of the ritual or on a specific angel. Damien Echols explains why he meditates before beginning a ritual: "Everything is made of energy—including our thoughts—and magick is about shaping and using energy. . . . [It] follows that we'd want to be more aware of that [thought] energy and the way it manifests."[35]

After centering the mind, a practitioner might want to scatter a few feathers, flowers, or other angelic symbols on the altar. Candles are arranged in a circle and lit while concentrating on a problem or wish. Wiccan practitioner Katherine Anne Lee uses these simple words to invite angels into her home after lighting candles: "Angels of love and beauty, I call upon you this day to help ease my burden. With your inspiring power and influence, show me the solutions I seek."[36]

Lee says she performed a ritual with those words when she desperately needed to find a new place to live. Within a week, Lee claims she had signed a lease on a house, her kids were enrolled in new schools, and she even received a cash windfall to pay for it all. Lee says her spells provided a strong focus for achieving her desires. But she still had to work hard to achieve success. She says:

> I have zero doubt that some serious angelic intervention was going on behind the scenes to make this not only happen unbelievably quickly, but without a hitch. It was as though opportunities were just dropping from the sky. It's not to say making any of this happen was easy, because it wasn't. . . . Even though it felt like life was accelerating for me, I was still in the driver's seat and I have to drive![37]

In addition to chanting spells, magicians might sing, dance, and drum during ceremonies. This is done with the intention of attaining a trancelike state that puts them in touch with the angels. Whichever method is used for summoning angels, the process can bring about a notable change in the person performing the ritual. Says RavenWolf, "You may find yourself surrounded by shining light and, as a result, become a shining being yourself, cloaked in the energies of the angel you have called."[38]

Reading the Cards

Wiccans sometimes use tarot cards during ceremonies as a way of calling on angels to foretell the future. The tarot deck consists of seventy-eight cards divided into two parts. The first twenty-two cards of the tarot are known as the major arcana. The minor arcana consists of fifty-six cards. (*Arcana* is Latin for "mysteries" or "secrets.") Each card in the major arcana has a number, picture, and name. Some of the cards, such as Strength and Justice, symbolize those universal themes. Others—including the Empress, the Hermit, and the Lovers—represent qualities typically associated with these characters.

Specific angels are associated with one or more of the major arcana cards. For example, Raphael is linked to the Magi-

Angels of the Major Arcana

People have used tarot cards for divination purposes since at least 1781. In the early twentieth century, members of a British occult society known as the Hermetic Order of the Golden Dawn linked each tarot card to one or more angels or archangels. Below are the cards of the major arcana, the angels associated with each card, and their meaning.

- 0. The Fool: Raphael, extravagance
- I. The Magician: Raphael (magic, enlightenment)
- II. The High Priestess: Gabriel (mystery, intuition)
- III. The Empress: Anael (fertility, mother)
- IV. The Emperor: Malkhidael (power, strength)
- V. The Hierophant: Asmodel (rituals, wisdom)
- VI. The Lovers: Ambriel (love, harmony)
- VII. The Chariot: Muriel (victory, travel)
- VIII. Strength: Zuriel (courage, action)
- IX. The Hermit: Hamaliel (solitude, loneliness)
- X. The Wheel of Fortune: Sachiel (destiny, luck)
- XI. Justice: Verkhiel (balance, harmony, law)
- XII. The Hanged Man: Gabriel (transition, suspension)
- XIII. Death: Barkhiel (regeneration, abrupt changes)
- XIV. Temperance: Adnakhiel (moderation, patience)
- XV. The Devil: Hanael (dishonesty, temptation)
- XVI. The Tower: Zamael (unexpected changes, adversity)
- XVII. The Star: Kambriel (hope, inspiration)
- XVIII. The Moon: Amnitziel (mystery, dreams)
- XIX. The Sun: Michael (satisfaction, love)
- XX. Judgment: Michael (forgiveness, rebirth)
- XXI. The World: Cassiel (perfection, success, eternal life)

cian card. "Raphael best represents the Magician, with his power over the winds, science, creativity, healing, [and] magickal tools," says RavenWolf. "When the Magician appears in your [tarot] reading look for a message from this blessed archangel."[39] Other angel–tarot card links include the High Priestess card and Uriel; the Moon card and Gabriel; and the Wheel of Fortune card and lesser-known angels such as Zachariel, Adabiel, and Sachiel.

Summoning angels with tarot cards is similar to performing ceremonial magic. Practitioners light candles and incense and concentrate intently on a problem or desire. When the mind is clear, the tarot deck is shuffled, and angels are summoned. Echols explains how the ritual is conducted:

Envision that a figure made of brilliant white light is standing next to your cards. You don't necessarily need to focus on the details of their appearance, but you know that the presence is angelic and there to help you. Inhale. See the angel grow brighter and brighter with each breath. Exhale and [speak] the angel's name. . . . Repeat the name as many times as you wish while focusing on the visualization and pulling in as much energy as feels necessary.[40]

When an angel appears to Echols, he asks it to provide blessings and power. After summoning the angel, he performs the tarot reading as he normally would. This is called throwing the tarot, a practice that involves laying the cards down in various patterns called spreads. The spread determines where each card goes and what

Using tarot cards, Wiccans sometimes call on angels to foretell the future. They might call on Raphael, who is associated with the Magician, or Uriel, who is associated with the High Priestess.

> "[Angel messengers] remind us of the importance of our spirituality and gently make it known in the [tarot] cards that our lives are refracted through a spiritual prism colored with unseen influences."[41]
>
> —Donna Hazel, tarot card reader

each card represents. The most basic pattern is called a three-card spread; three cards are laid out left to right. The first card symbolizes the past, the second the present, the third the future. Tarot card reader Donna Hazel provides her view on angelic tarot readings: "[Angel messengers] remind us of the importance of our spirituality and gently make it known in the cards that our lives are refracted through a spiritual prism colored with unseen influences. . . . The angels in the Tarot figure as a powerful invocation of that unseen spiritual world."[41]

Tarot decks contain a few cards, such as Death and the Devil, that can be rather unsettling when they turn up in readings. For this reason, some prefer to use what are called angel cards. Most angel card decks consist of around forty-five cards. Each card has a picture of an angel and an inspirational message. According to journalist Leo Giosuè, "Angel cards' focus is to provide gentle guidance from non-physical entities, especially from the angelic realm. . . . [Decks can include] fairies, goddesses, and any grouping considered spiritually evolved on the same level as Angels."[42]

Feeling Better

People seek gentle guidance from spiritual entities because the future is always unpredictable. For some, praying, meditating, and drawing on angels through magical ceremonies help make life more predictable. The rituals can also nourish the soul, delivering what Echols calls spiritual sustenance. For some, magic helps put daily distractions like social media, negative news events, and relationship problems in perspective. As Echols writes, "[The] benefit of gaining spiritual sustenance is that it . . . has profound effects on the physical realm: we feel lighter, happier, and more content; we also care a lot less about things that don't ultimately matter."[43]

Chapter Four

Devils and Demons

The Bible refers to the devil by thirty-three different names, including the Old Scratch, the Father of Lies, the Ruler of Darkness, Satan, and Lucifer. Many would shudder at the thought of communicating with the devil. But a Reddit poster with the username Mirta000 says he has invoked Lucifer over four hundred times. Mirta000 calls himself a Theistic Luciferian, someone who worships Lucifer as a god.

When Mirta000 contacts the devil, he says he experiences an enjoyable exchange of cosmic energy, what he calls "a stardust-like explosion."[44] Lucifer presents himself in the room as cold, heavy air, applying a strong pressure on Mirta000's upper arms, as if someone were holding him by the shoulders. Mirta000 says Lucifer enters his head and speaks in a male voice that is completely alien to his usual thoughts. According to Mirta000:

> A few times that I caught glimpses of him, once I saw him in a black mirror and he was a sharp faced man with dark hair and powerful eyes, another time in my dream I was playfully held down by grey hands with claws on them and my dream-self never looked at the face; once in a meditation vision I saw a bull-man. He shape shifts, so appearance is hard to describe, the cold, calm, peaceful aura is always the same though.[45]

Mirta000 says Lucifer is like most people, neither all good nor all bad. He believes the devil can help someone create trouble. But Lucifer might also encourage destructive impulses to teach him a lesson. Mirta000 says his contacts with Lucifer have provided him with emotional strength that allows him to live his life as he sees fit.

The Demon King, Prince, and Duke

Mirta000's concept of Lucifer stands in sharp contrast to the historical view of the devil and his demons. The New Testament depicts Satan as a dominant figure. He is called *diabolos*, which is a Greek term meaning "the slanderer." The biblical Satan is portrayed as an evil entity who commands a demon army that numbers in the hundreds of millions. Satan and his minions constantly tempt average people to sin and influence human affairs on a daily basis. The malevolent demons cause sickness, natural disasters, war, and death. Satan also reigns as the king of hell, a place where evildoers are said to burn in rivers of fire for eternity.

In 1467 a Spanish monk named Alfonso de Spina wrote that the demons of hell were part of a complex hierarchy. Spina was an expert in demonology, the study of demons. He wrote that demonic angels of various ranks created tempests, posed as false gods, deluded people into believing lies, and took revenge on innocents. Spina also concluded that demons in disguise persuaded humans to sin.

The book *Dictionnaire Infernal*, written by French occultist Jacques Collin de Plancy in 1818, is another source of demonology. The book includes names and descriptions of many fallen angels and their ranks in the demon hierarchy. The title page of the 1826 edition of *Dictionnaire Infernal* describes the content as "a Universal Library on . . . the manifestations and magic of trafficking with Hell; divinations, occult sciences, grimoires [spell books], marvels, errors, prejudices, traditions, folktales, the vari-

The biblical Satan (depicted in this stained-glass window) is portrayed as an evil being who commands a demon army. Satan and his minions are said to be constantly wreaking havoc wherever and whenever they can.

ous superstitions, and generally all manner of marvellous, surprising, mysterious, and supernatural beliefs."[46]

Collin de Plancy gave demons aristocratic titles similar to those of nobles and military commanders who wielded power in human society. He refers to the demon Astaroth as the Great Duke of Hell. Astaroth is a fallen angel who rides a dragon and

An Encounter with the Demon Semyaza

Many times descriptions of demonic encounters sound like horror stories. And sometimes horror stories trigger demonic encounters. This was the case with a witch named Saroya, who says her nighttime encounter with the demon Semyaza was triggered after seeing the film *It*, based on the Stephen King horror novel. *It* features an eyeless dancing clown named Pennywise whose mouth is filled with razor-sharp teeth.

Saroya says that after watching *It* in 2019, she awoke in the middle of the night to the sounds of whispering and chanting. Her bed was surrounded by at least seven demons that resembled Pennywise. Two nights later the Pennywise demons appeared once again and took Saroya to a portal surrounded by flames and stars. Saroya picks up the story: "[The portal] looked like some sort of cavern deep within the Earth's core and there were all these undead-looking, grey and black figures with angel-like wings. . . . It was then that I realized these were Semyaza's warriors . . . [with] multiple arms and blood red eyes. One of these arms held a long, very menacing-looking spear." Saroya joined the demons to battle a second group of undead entities until all were vanquished.

Saroya, "Shub-Niggurath, Semyaza and the Watchers," *Dancing Corpse Witch* (blog), September 21, 2019. https://dancingcorpsewitch.wordpress.com.

carries a viper in his right hand. Like several other fallen angels, Astaroth believes he was unjustly punished by God and will someday return to his rightful place in heaven. Astaroth is known for his impressive wisdom and deadly halitosis, as a blogger with the username Prof. Geller writes:

> It is said that when Astaroth is summoned, he is willing to share his great knowledge of the past, present, future, and intellectual pursuits. However . . . his foul smelling breath . . . is said to be fatal upon encounters. To protect oneself from Astaroth's breath, it is said that a charmed ring made of pure silver can be used as protection. This ring must be held underneath the nose of the summoner to ensure that the individual will remain protected for the entire interaction with Astaroth. Failure to do this will result in death.[47]

Collin de Plancy calls the demon Azazel a fearsome prince of hell and a seducer of humankind. Azazel has seven serpent heads, fourteen faces, and twelve wings. He was cast from heaven for failing to bow down when the first human, Adam, was presented to God. The apocryphal book of Enoch says Azazel instructed men on ways to make weapons and showed women how to use cosmetics. "[Azazel taught women the] beautifying of the eyelids; and all kinds of costly stones and all coloring tinctures. And there arose much godlessness, and they . . . were led astray and became corrupt in all their ways."[48]

> "[Astaroth's] foul smelling breath . . . is said to be fatal upon encounters. To protect oneself . . . it is said that a charmed ring made of pure silver can be used as protection."[47]
>
> —Prof. Geller, blogger

In Dictionnaire Infernal, the demon Astaroth (pictured) is portrayed as a fallen angel who rides a dragon and carries a viper in his right hand. Astaroth believes he was unjustly punished by God and will someday return to his rightful place in heaven.

Devious Demons

Semyaza is the leader of the Watchers, a name given to angels who observe the activities of people on earth. Watchers can be bad or good; those associated with Semyaza are fallen angels. They mated with human women who gave birth to a race of brutal giants called Nephilim. The half-angel, half-human creatures are so hungry that every day a single Nephilim eats one thousand camels, one thousand horses, and one thousand oxen. In addition to their sinful couplings, wicked Watchers teach humans how to practice magic, astrology, and alchemy (the mystical process that purports to turn lead into gold).

The demon Beelzebub is known as the prince of all dark princes and said to have powers second only to Satan's. In heaven he was the highest-ranking angel. After his fall, Beelzebub became the chief of demons. He resembles a giant fly and bears the nickname Lord of the Flies.

Mephistopheles, whose name in Greek means "he who loves not the light," is another powerful prince of hell closely associated with Satan. But while Satan appears with cloven hooves, horns,

Demon Warning Signs

The Bible contains stories about adults and children who experienced demonic possession. These tales have inspired countless stories about evil spirits that take control of innocent people. Many are skeptical that demonic possession is real. But those who have studied possession say it is possible to recognize the presence of demons.

Those who believe that they have encountered demons often report feeling a powerful dark energy force surrounding them, as if they were being watched by a malevolent entity. This is often accompanied by involuntary physical reactions such as goose bumps, chills, or hair standing up on the back of the neck. A horrid sulfurious smell might fill the air, causing nausea or sudden illness. Inexplicable sounds such as a knocking, growling, or low murmurs are another sign that a demon is nearby.

Some people are actually possessed by demons. They become extremely hateful and behave like rabid animals. The possessed might hiss, spit, and foam at the mouth, and a growling voice speaks through them. In such cases a priest might be called in to conduct an exorcism, which involves casting out the demon(s) through prayer and ritual.

and a tail, Mephistopheles resembles a human. This demon has been depicted in numerous works of art, books, TV shows, and films as a tall, suave man dressed in black from head to toe. These stories usually focus on people who strike a bargain with Mephistopheles to sell their souls in exchange for money, love, power, and fame. Mephistopheles is said to carry a red book with contracts for sinners to sign away their souls.

Those who sign the red book of Mephistopheles have their signatures notarized by Baal, hell's master of rituals and pacts. Baal was once a high god and lord of life. But he engaged in a battle with death and was sent to hell. Baal appears with three heads, that of a toad, a man, and a cat. Black magicians who wish to become invisible invoke his name.

The Bluesman and the Devil

In one of the most famous tales about someone selling his soul to the devil, Mephistopheles and the devil are portrayed as one and the same. The legend is based on the life of the influential blues musician Robert Johnson, born in Mississippi in 1911. Johnson traveled the South strumming his guitar and singing on street corners and saloon stages. According to legend, he met up with the devil at a crossroads south of Rosedale, Mississippi, around 1931. At the time, Johnson was an unknown musician who was so bad he was rebuked by blues legend Son House, who said, "Put that guitar down, boy, you drivin' people nuts."[49]

Dejected, penniless, and in need of a drink, Johnson was walking down the lonely Highway 8 with his guitar slung over his shoulder. Where the highway crossed Dockery Road, Johnson saw a sick dog moaning in the ditch and a strange man sitting on a log. The man said Johnson was late for his appointment. Sensing the man's supernatural presence, Johnson fell down on his knees. Rosedale resident Henry Goodman picks up the story: "[The devil said] stand up, Robert Johnson. You want to throw that guitar over there in that ditch . . . because you just another guitar player like all the rest, or you want to play that guitar like nobody ever played it before? Make a sound nobody ever heard before? You want to be the King of the Delta Blues and have all the whiskey and women you want?"[50]

As the devil finished talking, Johnson saw the moon growing and expanding until he felt the heat of it searing his neck like the noonday sun of summer. The dog let out a low, rhythmic moan that penetrated every nerve in Johnson's body. He could feel the moan vibrating in his heart and shaking his entire being. This caused the strings of Johnson's guitar to vibrate in a soulful and darkly beautiful melody. Johnson then had an out-of-body experience. Floating above the scene, the bluesman realized the dog was a hellhound working with the devil.

Johnson finally found his voice: "I got to have that sound, Devil-Man. That sound is mine. Where do I sign?"[51] The Devil replied:

> Your word is good enough. All you got to do is keep walking north. But you better be prepared. There are consequences. . . . You are going to have the Blues like never known to this world. My left hand will be forever wrapped around your soul, and your music will possess all who hear it. That's what's going to happen. That's what you better be prepared for. Your soul will belong to me. Go on, Robert Johnson. You the King of the Delta Blues.[52]

Johnson went on to achieve fame with his epic combination of singing, guitar playing, and songwriting skills. The albums he recorded in 1936 and 1937 produced songs that influenced some of the biggest names in 1960s and 1970s rock and roll, including Jimi Hendrix, the Beatles, the Rolling Stones, Eric Clapton, and Led Zeppelin. However, Johnson met his end in 1938 at a rural crossroads similar to the place where he is rumored to have met the devil.

Johnson was only twenty-seven when he died. Some say he was poisoned by his lover's jealous husband, while others say

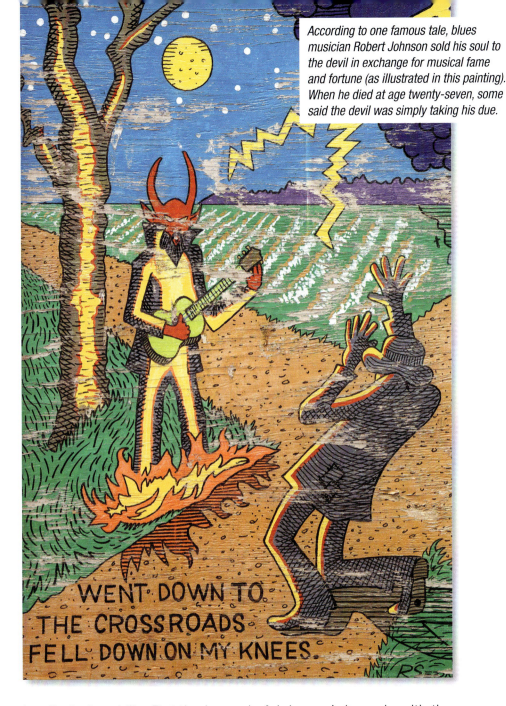

According to one famous tale, blues musician Robert Johnson sold his soul to the devil in exchange for musical fame and fortune (as illustrated in this painting). When he died at age twenty-seven, some said the devil was simply taking his due.

he died of syphilis. But the legend of Johnson's bargain with the devil has lived on along with his music. And many still believe that when Johnson died, the devil was simply taking his due and collecting the soul the guitar player had traded away many years before.

Incubus Attacks

Another type of nighttime encounter with dark forces is so common that it has a name: the incubus phenomenon. *Incubus* is Latin for "nightmare induced by a demon." The term is commonly used for a male demon; a female demon is called a succubus (one who lies under). When the incubus phenomenon occurs, a person will wake up in the middle of the night with a sense of dread, feeling as if they are being attacked by a demon. Victims are paralyzed and have a hard time breathing. They feel as if a demon is sitting on their chest. They are unable to scream or run away. Incubus attacks have been reported in the United States, England, China, Japan, and elsewhere. According to a 2017 study by researchers in Netherlands, around one in ten people experience the incubus phenomenon at least once in their lifetimes. While it is often dismissed as a bad dream, the phenomenon can cause anxiety and insomnia.

Blogger Chrissy Stockton describes a high school junior who was attacked by an incubus. Like many who believe they have had nighttime encounters with demons, the girl wishes to remain anonymous. Stockton writes that the girl was sleeping in her bed when she awoke to find a shadowy figure standing in the middle of the room staring at her. The being let out a growl that turned into a high-pitched hiss. According to the girl:

> As it made this hissing sound it raised its arms up and what I can only describe as claw like fingers grew longer and longer until they reached across and down through my body. The feeling was unlike anything I have ever experienced before and every part of my body that it was ripping through felt a dead cold burn that registered absolute hopelessness and lifelessness, a very horrible and unequal feeling. Again the shadow let out the unforgettable hiss while it lifted its arms again, reaching out and clawing through me again . . . and again, and again.[53]

The girl said she prayed and used spiritual energy to push the incubus away. As the demon fought back, it grabbed hold of a crucifix the girl always wore on a gold chain around her neck. She heard a snap and felt the crucifix fall off. The shadowy demon then began to fade until it disappeared. The exhausted girl instantly fell into a deep sleep. In the morning she thought what she had experienced was only a nightmare. But when she reached for her crucifix, she noticed it was on the floor. She says:

> "As it made this hissing sound it raised its arms up and what I can only describe as claw like fingers grew longer and longer until they reached across and down through my body."[53]
>
> —Anonymous victim of demon attack

> As the reflection of the cross and broken chain shined back towards me my heart was now pounding out of my chest because it was clear physical evidence to me that what I had experienced the night before was not a dream that felt undeniably real but an event with physical evidence. To this day it was one of the most terrifying and mysterious moments of my life. I strongly feel like I was able to defeat the evil shadow with sheer will and faith.[54]

People Believe

Psychologists say people might believe they have been attacked by malevolent spirits, but there is no scientific evidence to prove such spirits are real. However, a 2023 Gallup poll showed that around 60 percent of Americans believe in the devil. That translates to tens of millions of people who think Lucifer fell from heaven to torment humanity.

While people seem to encounter angels more often than demons, their experiences with the devil represent the age-old battle between good and evil. This contrast has been portrayed in the folklore of almost every culture and has provided inspiration for countless creative works. This has kept the devil at the forefront of human imagination for centuries. And as long as the ultimate monster continues to haunt people night and day, the devil will not disappear but will continue to walk the earth with his army of demons.

Source Notes

Introduction: Spirits in the Sky

1. Peter 2:11 (English Standard Version).
2. Quoted in Judy Lekic, *Angelic Intervention: Tools for Healing*. Bloomington, IN: Balboa, 2014, p. 89.
3. Gabby Bernstein, "An Introduction to the 7 Archangels and Guardian Angels," Gabby Bernstein (personal website), 2023. https://gabbybernstein.com.

Chapter One: Everlasting Angels

4. Ezekiel 10:12 (New Revised Standard Version).
5. Shawna Smith, "Biblically Accurate Angels Are Crucial in Modern Media," Study Breaks, December 21, 2022. https://studybreaks.com.
6. Quoted in David Crary, "Ancient but Small in Number, Zoroastrians Confront Depletion of Their Faith," *PBS NewsHour*, July 1, 2022. www.pbs.org.
7. Doreen Virtue, *Archangels 101*. Carlsbad, CA: Hay House, 2010, p. xiv.
8. Hebrews 13:2 (Christian Standard Bible).
9. Revelation 8:7 (New International Version).
10. Daniel N. Geffen, "The Power and Protection of Angels," Union for Reform Judaism, 2023. https://reformjudaism.org.

Chapter Two: Guardian Angels

11. Exodus 32:34 (New International Version).
12. Quoted in Richard Longo, "Did You Know You Are Protected 24/7?," Catholic Diocese of Pittsburgh, October 26, 2021. https://diopitt.org.
13. Quoted in Georges Huber, "The Role of Guardian Angels in Our Lives," Catholic Culture, 2023. www.catholicculture.org.
14. Hope Lux, "Angel Visits: 6 Signs That Archangel Michael Is Around You," *The Angel Writer* (blog), 2023. www.theangelwriter.com/blog/signs-archangel-michael.

15. Bernstein, "An Introduction to the 7 Archangels and Guardian Angels."
16. Quoted in Lux, "Angel Visits."
17. Doreen Virtue, "Healing Miracles from Archangel Raphael," Beliefnet, 2022. www.beliefnet.com.
18. Wille, "6 Powerful Signs of Archangel Raphael You Need to Recognize," *A Little Spark of Joy* (blog), July 12, 2023. www.alittlesparkofjoy.com.
19. Stacey, "Who Is Archangel Ariel? The Angel of Mother Earth," Black Feather Intuitive, 2023. www.theblackfeatherintuitive.com.
20. Stacey, "Who Is Archangel Ariel?"
21. Quoted in Whitney Hopler, "How to Recognize Archangel Gabriel," Learn Religions, February 8, 2021. www.learnreligions.com.
22. Lynda, "Archangel Uriel: Signs That Archangel Uriel Is Around You," *Whatever Your Dose* (blog), May 29, 2023. https://whateveryourdose.com.
23. Quoted in Paul, "The Empowering Flame of Archangel Uriel," *Psychic Bloggers*, May 26, 2023. https://psychicbloggers.com.
24. Quoted in Melissa Brinks, "15 People Tell Eerie Stories of Guardian Angels Looking Out for Them," Ranker, March 2, 2021. www.ranker.com.
25. Quoted in Brinks, "15 People Tell Eerie Stories of Guardian Angels Looking Out for Them."
26. Quoted in Barbara Diamond, "Woman Sees 'Guardian Angel' Seconds After Slamming into a Pole," Little Things, January 7, 2016. https://littlethings.com.
27. Quoted in Diamond, "Woman Sees 'Guardian Angel' Seconds After Slamming into a Pole."

Chapter Three: Harnessing Angelic Energy

28. Quoted in Carey Dunne, "Magick 'Saved My Life': The Former Death Row Inmate Turned Warlock," *The Guardian* (Manchester, UK), October 27, 2018. www.theguardian.com.
29. Quoted in Dunne, "Magick 'Saved My Life.'"
30. Jenny Smedley, "Angels in Paganism," Dante Mag, 2023. www.dantemag.com.
31. Silver RavenWolf, *Angels: Companions in Magick*. St. Paul, MN: Llewellyn, 2003, p. 16.
32. RavenWolf, *Angels*, p. 19.

33. Quoted in Tess Whitehurst, "Angels and Magick—the Perspectives of Two Very Different Witches," *Witches & Pagans*, August 14, 2014. https://witchesandpagans.com.
34. Whoismyguardianangel, "Virgo and Archangel Metatron," Tumbler, 2023. www.tumblr.com.
35. Damien Echols, *Angels & Archangels: A Magician's Guide*. Boulder, CO: Sounds True, 2020, p. 162.
36. Katherine Anne Lee, "Angels + Magic? Hell Yeah! Here's What You Need to Know About Angelic Witchcraft!," Numerologist, April 6, 2019. https://numerologist.com.
37. Lee, "Angels + Magic?"
38. RavenWolf, *Angels*, p. 21.
39. RavenWolf, *Angels*, p. 248.
40. Damien Echols, *High Magick*. Boulder, CO: Sounds True, 2018, p. 173.
41. Donna Hazel, "Angels in the Tarot Cards with Donna Hazel," Biddy Tarot, 2023. www.biddytarot.com.
42. Leo Giosuè, "What Is the Difference Between Tarot, Oracle Cards, and Angel Cards?," *Jerusalem Post*, March 31, 2021. www.jpost.com.
43. Echols, *Angels & Archangels*, p. 5.

Chapter Four: Devils and Demons

44. Mirta000, "Looking for True Encounters with Demons," Reddit, 2022. www.reddit.com.
45. Mirta000, "Looking for True Encounters with Demons."
46. Quoted in Eric Grundhauser, "The Best Demon Illustrations of All Time," Atlas Obscura, July 10, 2017. www.atlasobscura.com.
47. Prof. Geller, "Astaroth," Mythology.net, 2022. https://mythology.net.
48. "1 Enoch 8:1," 2023. https://intertextual.bible.
49. Quoted in Henry Goodman, "Meeting with the Devil at the Crossroads," *Mr. Rickman's Blog*, September 2017. https://rickmanhchs.files.wordpress.com.
50. Goodman, "Meeting with the Devil at the Crossroads."
51. Goodman, "Meeting with the Devil at the Crossroads."
52. Goodman, "Meeting with the Devil at the Crossroads."
53. Quoted in Chrissy Stockton, "11 True Stories of People's Terrifying Encounters with Evil," Thought Catalog, October 31, 2014. https://thoughtcatalog.com.
54. Quoted in Stockton, "11 True Stories of People's Terrifying Encounters with Evil."

For Further Research

Books

Damien Echols, *Angels & Archangels: A Magician's Guide*. Boulder, CO: Sounds True, 2020.

Esther J. Hamori, *God's Monsters: Vengeful Spirits, Deadly Angels, Hybrid Creatures, and Divine Hitmen of the Bible*. Minneapolis: Broadleaf, 2023.

Carol K. Mack and Dinah Mack, *A Field Guide to Demons, Vampires, Fallen Angels, and Other Subversive Spirits*. New York: Arcade, 2021.

Jason Miller, *Consorting with Spirits: Your Guide to Working with Invisible Allies*. New York: Weiser, 2022.

Edward Simon, *Pandemonium: A Visual History of Demonology*. New York: Cernunnos, 2022.

Internet Sources

Jamie Ballard and Ysolt Usigan, "What Are Angel Numbers? A Guide to Their Special Meaning," *Woman's Day*, March 28, 2023. www.womansday.com.

Gabby Bernstein, "An Introduction to the 7 Archangels and Guardian Angels," Gabby Bernstein (personal website), 2023. https://gabbybernstein.com.

Melissa Brinks, "15 People Tell Eerie Stories of Guardian Angels Looking Out for Them," Ranker, March 2, 2021. www.ranker.com.

Hope Lux, "Angel Visits: 6 Signs That Archangel Michael Is Around You," *The Angel Writer* (blog), 2023. www.theangelwriter.com.

Jenny Smedley, "Angels in Paganism," Dante Mag, 2023. www.dantemag.com.

Websites

Angelicpedia
https://angelicpedia.com
Names of angels from A to Z are provided by this site, which also has biographies of archangels, fallen angels, and others from Christianity, Judaism, and Islam.

Beliefnet
www.beliefnet.com
This website focuses on religious beliefs and features information about angels, along with stories from those who claim to have encountered angels.

DeliriumsRealm
www.deliriumsrealm.com
This website provides information about demons and demonology. The site's Demon Database covers malevolent supernatural spirits from many religions and cultures, from the Americas and Asia to Europe and the Middle East.

Mythology.net
https://mythology.net
This website features comprehensive descriptions of angels, demons, monsters, and other legendary creatures from ancient mythologies, including Greek, Egyptian, and others.

Satanic Temple
https://thesatanictemple.com
Members of the Satanic Temple do not worship Satan but view him as a character who battles repression, promotes religious tolerance, and acts with empathy toward all creatures. The group's website covers current events, the group's ministry, and advocacy services.

Index

Note: Boldface page numbers indicate illustrations.

Abrahamic religions, 6
   Zoroastrianism as basis for monotheism of, 6
Adabiel (angel), 40
Ahura Mazda (Persian deity), 10–11
Aladdin, **18**, 19
altars, Wiccan, 34–35
Amesha Spenta (Zoroastrian archangels), 11
Angelicpedia (website), 58
angels
   in angelic hierarchy, 16
   archangels *vs.*, 38
   biblical hierarchy of, 12–13
   in book of Revelation, 16–17
   as comic characters, 4
   computer images of, 8–9, **9**
   gender of, 11
   as influence in modern world, 6–7
   of Islam, 17–19
   linked with tarot cards, 39–40
   as messengers, 7, 9–10, 19, 42
   portrayal in art, 8, 11
   prevalence of belief in, 7
   unnamed, as protectors, 27–31
   Zoroastrian, 11
Angels & Archangels (Echols), 33
Angels of Pure Contemplation (angelic triad), 14
Angels of the Cosmos (angelic triad), 15
Angels of the World (angelic triad), 15–16
Apocryphal texts, 15–16, 35
Aquinas, Thomas, 6, 13, **13**
Arabian Nights, The, **18**, 19
archangels, 4, 15–16
   angels *vs.*, 38
   in Islam, 17
   linked with tarot cards, 39–40
   as messengers, 15, 16
   in Persian culture, 10–11
   Zoroastrian, 10, 11
Ariel (archangel), 24–25, 35
   in Wiccan religion, 35
art
   Gabriel portrayed in, 11, 26, **27**
   Mephistopheles portrayed in, 49
   Michael portrayed in, 4, **5**
   portrayal of angels in, 8, 9–10, 11
Asha Vahishta (Zoroastrian archangel), 11
Astaroth (demon), 45–46, **47**

Azazel (demon), 46–47

Baal (demon), 49
Bahá'í faith, 6
Beelzebub (demon), 48
Beliefnet (website), 58
Bernstein, Gabby, 6, 22
Bible, 6, 12–13
   archangel Gabriel in, 25
   archangel Michael in, 21
   demonic possession in, 48
   description of angels in, 4, 11, 16
   references to the devil in, 43
   See also New Testament; Old Testament

Celts, 33
Chasan (angel), 36
cherubim, 8, 14
   in Islam, 17
Choksy, Jamsheed, 12
Christianity, Zoroastrianism as basis for monotheism of, 6
Collin de Plancy, Jacques, 44–46

DC Universe, 4
DeliriumsRealm (website), 58
demons
   hierarchy of, 44–47
   in Jewish folklore, 6
   possession by, 48
devas (Hindu angels), 14
Dictionnaire Infernal (Collin de Plancy), 44–45
djinni (Islamic angels), 17–19, **18**
dominions (angelic class), 15

Echols, Damien, 32–33, 38, 40–41
Egyptian deities, 10
Elaine Belloc (comic book character), 4
Ezekiel (prophet), 8

Gabriel (archangel), 25
   artistic portrayal of, 11, 26, **27**
   link with tarot cards, 40
   as messenger, 15, 16
   role in Islam, 17
   in Wiccan religion, 36
Gallup poll, 7
Geffen, Daniel N., 19
Giosuè, Leo, 42
Goodman, Henry, 49–50
good *vs.* evil, battle between, 7, 11–12
   in folklore, 53
   role of angels in, 16
   in Zoroastrianism, 11–12

Hanks, Hunter, 29–30, 31
Hazel, Donna, 42
Hermetic Order of the Golden Dawn (British occult society), 40
Hinduism, 14
Hopler, Whitney, 14

incubus (demon), 52
Isis (Egyptian deity), 10
Islam
   angels of, 17–19
   Zoroastrianism as basis for monotheism of, 6
Israfil (archangel), 17
It (King), 46

Izra'il (archangel), 17

Jerome (saint), 20
Jesus, 12, 16
Jewish folklore, demons in, 6
Jibril, 17
  See also Gabriel
Johnson, Robert, 49–51, **51**
John the Evangelist, 16, 17
Judaism, Zoroastrianism as basis for monotheism of, 6

King, Stephen, 46
Koran, 17
  archangel Michael in, 21

Lee, Katherine Anne, 38–39
light, spiritual meaning of, 14
Lucifer, 43–44
  See also Satan
Lux, Hope, 22

Maat (Egyptian deity), 10
Marvel Cinematic Universe, 4
Mary, 16
Mephistopheles (demon), 48–49
Metatron (archangel), 36–37, **37**
Michael Demiurgos (comic book archangel), 4
Michael the Archangel, 15
  artistic portrayal of, 4, **5**
  in fight with Satan, 17
  as guardian angel, 21–22
  in Wiccan religion, 36
Miller-Russo, Linda, 26
Miller-Russo, Peter, 26
Moriel (angel), 36
Moses, 20, **21**

Muhammad the Prophet, 17
Mythology.net, 58

Nephilim (giants), 48
New Testament, 12
  archangels in, 16
  depiction of Satan in, 5, 44

Old Testament, 20
  archangels/principalities in, 15
opinion polls. *See* surveys

pagans/neo-pagans, 33
Peart, Amanda, 23
Pius XII (pope), 20–21
polls. *See* surveys
powers (angelic class), 15
principalities (angelic class), 15
Prophet Muhammad, 17

Raphael (archangel), 15
  as healing angel, 22–24
  link with tarot cards, 39–40
  in Wiccan religion, 36
RavenWolf, Silver, 35
Revelation, book of, 16–17

Sachiel (angel), 40
Satan, 5, **45**
  biblical references to, 43
Satanic Temple, 58
Semyaza (demon), 46, 48
seraphim, 11, 14
Sikhism, 6
Smedley, Jenny, 33
Smith, Shawna, 9
Spina, Alfonso de, 44
Stockton, Chrissy, 52

Stonehenge, **34**
Stovall, Arika, 29, 30–31
succubus (demon), 52
Sumer/Sumerian art, 9–10
surveys
   on belief in angels, 7
   on belief in devil, 53
   on belief in guardian angels, 20

Tanakh (Hebrew Bible), 12
tarot cards, 39–42, 41
thrones (angelic class), 14

Uriel (archangel), 16
   artistic portrayal of, 26, **27**
   in Wiccan religion, 35–36

Vedas (Hindu religious texts), 14
Virtue, Doreen, 14, 23–24

virtues (angelic class), 15
Vohu Manah (Zoroastrian archangel), 10

Watchers, 48
Wauters, Ambika, 26
Wicca, 33
   four elements and, 35–37
   practices of, 33–35

Zachariel (angel), 40
Zarathustra. *See* Zoroaster
Zauriel (comic book angel), 4
Zoroaster (Zarathustra, Persian mystic), 10
Zoroastrianism, 10–11
   number of people practicing, 11
   seraphim and, 14

Picture Credits

Cover: Daniel Eskridge/Stock

5: Linda McKusick/Shutterstock
9: Love Employee/Shutterstock
13: Renata Sedmakova/Shutterstock
18: Hilary Morgan/Alamy Stock Photo
21: Lebrecht Music & Arts/Alamy Stock Photo
27: Jim Holden/Alamy Stock Photo
28: Cormac Price/Shutterstock
34: Walker Art Library/Alamy Stock Photo
37: Panther Media GmbH/Alamy Stock Photo
41: Charles Walker Collection/Alamy Stock Photo
45: Andrew Wood/Alamy Stock Photo
47: Stefano Bianchetti/Bridgeman Images
51: Hemis/Alamy Stock Photo

About the Author

Stuart A. Kallen is the author of more than 350 nonfiction books for children and young adults. He has written on topics ranging from the theory of relativity to the art of electronic dance music. In 2018 Kallen won a Green Earth Book Award from the Nature Generation environmental organization for his book *Trashing the Planet: Examining the Global Garbage Glut*. In his spare time he is a singer, songwriter, and guitarist in San Diego.